Thank you God for Loving Me

Gracias Dios por Amarme

Illustrated and written by

Grace Young

WestBow Press books may be ordered through booksellers or by contacting:

WestBow Press
A Division of Thomas Nelson & Zondervan
1663 Liberty Drive
Bloomington, IN 47403
www.westbowpress.com
844-714-3454

All scripture quotations are taken from the King James Version

ISBN: 979-8-3850-1345-6 (sc)
ISBN: 979-8-3850-1346-3 (e)

Library of Congress Control Number: 2023922704

Print information available on the last page.

WestBow Press rev. date: 01/29/2024

WESTBOW
PRESS®
A DIVISION OF THOMAS NELSON
& ZONDERVAN

This book is dedicated to David,
Christopher, Josh, Michelle, Brianna, Isaiah,
Athena Marie, Meira Simone, Mia Skye,
Malana Serah, Minah Sommer, and
my mother, Local Preacher,
Mrs. Grace E. Williams.

Thank you God for Loving Me is a story about a little boy, who is now a grown up young man. He remembers how God had blessed him as a young boy. He truly knows now that when he was young it was God who was blessing him all the long. He has a sister who grew up to be a beautiful young lady. They both got married and had families of their own.

His baby brother grew up and he became a preacher. The young man wanted his children to learn early in their young lives, about how good God is. He started teaching his children about some things that they should be thankful for.

He is also very thankful now how God has blessed him with new family members.

Gracias Dios por amarme, es una historia acerca de un niño, Quien crecio para ser un joven adulto. El recuerda como Dios lo bendijo cuando era niño. Ahora reconoce cuando era niño, fue Dios quien siempre lo bendijo. El tiene una hermana que creció hacer una hermosa Señorita. Los dos están Casados y cada uno tiene su propia familia.

Su hermano pequeño se convirtió en un pastor. Este Joven queria que sus hijos aprendieran desde muy niños de las Bendiciones de Dios. El empezó a enseñarles a sus hijos a dar gracias por las cosas que ellos deberián estar agradecidos por.

El ahora también esta agradecido de como Dios lo ha Bendecido con nuevos miembros en su familia.

Thank you God for the pretty yellow sun.

Gracias Dios per el hermoso sol amarillo.

Thank you God for the
pretty blue sky.

Gracias Dios por el
hermoso cielo azul.

Thank you God for the beautiful
birds singing in the trees.

Gracias Dios por los
pajaros hermosos que
cantan en los árboles.

Thank you God for all the beautiful flowers.

Gracias Dios por todas las flores hermosas.

Thank you God
for all the trees.

Gracias Dios por
todos los árboles.

Thank you God for my brother.

Our Father, who art in heaven
hallowed be thy name; thy
Kingdom come thy will be
done...(Matthew 6:9-13 KJV)

Gracias Dios por mi hermano.

Thank you God for my sister,
niece and nephew.

Gracias Dios por mi hermana,
mi sobrina y mi sobrino.

Thank you God for my
Brother-in-Law who
has a job to protect and
serve the people.

Gracias Dios por mi Cuñado
que tiene el trabajo de
proteger y servir a la gente.

Thank you God for my mother and father.

Gracias Dios por mi mamá y mi papá.

Thank you God for my cat.

Gracias Dios por mi gato.

Thank you God
for the good food
that we eat.

Gracias Dios por la comida que comemos.

Thank you God for my church.

Gracias Dios por mi Iglesia.

Thank you God for my children.

Gracias Dios por mis hijos.

Thank you God for my wife.

Gracias Dios por mi esposa.

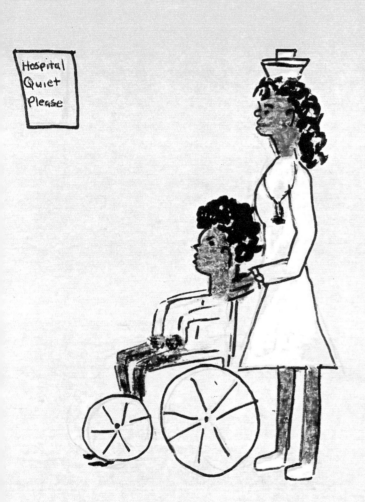

Thank you God for the
doctors and nurses.

Gracias Dios por los
doctores y las enfermeras.

Thank you God for the clothes that we wear.

Gracias Dios por la ropa que usamos.

Thank you God for my car.

Gracias Dios por mi carro.

Thank you God for my house.

Gracias Dios por mi casa.

Thank you God for my school.

Gracias Dios por mi escuela.

Thank you God for loving me
because your Son, Jesus,
died on the cross to save me.

Gracias Dios por amarme porque tu hijo
Jesus, murio en la Cruz para salvarme.

About Grace Young

She is an experienced teacher who has been involved in the education of children for many years. She knows that children should be taught with simple and plain vocabulary that they can understand. She is also the author of another book, Why I Thank God. She is also very aware that illustrations are very important in bringing a point across. The illustrations should be colorful as well as interesting.

She has earned the following degrees: Bachelor's Degree in Psychology with minor in Elementary Education and a Master of Science Degree in Education (Reading). She also holds permanent certificates in Education and Reading from the College of New Rochelle in New Rochelle, New York, and a certificate of Theology from Oral Roberts University in Tulsa, Oklahoma. She also earned an A.A.S. Degree in Nursing from Pace University in Pleasantville, New York. She also graduated with a Preachers License from Charis Bible College, Beacon, New York in May 2023.

"For God so loved the world, that He gave His only begotten Son, that whosoever believeth in Him should not perish, but have everlasting life." (John 3:16 KJV)

"Porque de tal manera amó Dios al mundo, que ha dado a su Hijo unigenito, para que todo aquel que en él cree, no se pierda, mas tenga vida eterna." (John 3:16 KJV)

Printed in the United States
by Baker & Taylor Publisher Services